THE RESTORATION OF FASTING AND PRAYER

The Restoration of Fasting and Prayer

CHIEF APOSTLE JOSEPH PRUDE

RESTORATION OF FASTING & PRAYER

CONTENTS

THE RESTORATION OF FASTING AND PRAYER

When you fast, you bring your spirit into a place which allows you to receive revelation. One thing you want to always remember is that revelation comes out of your spirit. You want to bring your soul and your mind into a place of quietness as you fast, then you are positioned so that your spirit-man is able to receive. This is just one form of how revelation comes.

When Peter fasted and pressed through to the revelation of God's purposes in the church, it allowed him to take the church into the new era. This only came about because of fasting and prayer.

Our objective is not so much to discuss techniques, although we will discuss some, but to understand why prayer, supplication and fasting are so important to you, your family and to the church! Since we have spent such a great deal of time looking at the life and ministry of Jesus, in the gospels, then it should behoove us, the church, to see the biblical patterns that Christ, Himself, has already established for us to follow.

It is my prayer that this book and it's "Holy-Spirit-given" message will release something into the body of Christ, as well as into your personal life. This will help spark the harvest of this end time, as you prayerfully read this book. I believe many traditions will come down and the liberty of Jesus Christ will come forth.

Apostle Joseph Prude

THE RESTORATION OF FASTING AND PRAYER

We are in an hour of restoration. The Lord is bringing a restoration to the truths that satan has deceived the church into disregarding. Fasting and prayer happens to be one of these truths and there is a great need of this restoration in this day and time.

Every great move of God has always been preceded by prayer and fasting. Jesus began His ministry after a time of fasting and prayer, (Luke 4:1,2). Peter went unto the gentiles after fasting, (Acts 10:10). Cornelius received the gospel and became the first gentile to be saved after fasting, (Acts 10:30). Moses lead the children of Israel through the wilderness and received the Law after he fasted, (Exodus 34:28). Elijah received strength to continue his ministry after fasting, (2 Kings 19:8). Paul began his ministry after fasting, (Acts 9:9).

Every re-direction of a change, by the spirit, is preceded by fasting. In these recent times we can recall the William Branhams, the Oral Roberts, the A.A. Allens, and the T.L. Osborns of this day and age. These were men and women of God that greatly affected their generation through prayer and fasting. In this book, we will attempt to share with you the truths of fasting, as we are led of the spirit. We have just come through a season in which we have witnessed the move of "positive confession" being re-established, as it pertains to the Word. Praise God for that move, but we must now go on.

The Bible says in Hebrews 6:1, "LET US GO ON UNTO PERFECTION," (emphasis, per author). Praise God! The fact of the matter is that the confession of the Word can only bring life. It is the Word that is confessing Himself through us, (John 1:14), "...AND THE WORD BECAME FLESH," (emphasis, per author). Now the flesh must become the Word. This therefore means that the confession is no longer you or I, but it is the Living Word speaking through us. Thus, we must die to ourselves, so that He might live in us!

CHAPTER ONE

WHAT IS FASTING?

The process of death to self is best accomplished through fasting. We will, therefore, take a look at fasting as it relates to the purposes of God.

The word "fast" means - TO ABSTAIN! When we fast, we are in a period of abstinence. We better understand what it means to fast, when we think in terms of the word "abstinence". The word abstinence is the notion of shutting oneself off from that which satisfies the soul, (Isaiah 58:6), "...Is not this the fast I have chosen? A day for a man to afflict his soul..." (KJV). The desire for food, sex and gratification are all connected to the soulical realm. To afflict the soul, is to tell oneself - NO! We must begin to understand the overall concept of fasting is more than to just abstain from the consumption of food. Yes, a food fast is what is most commonly spoken of as it pertains to fasting, but that is certainly not all of it.

God's first ordained fast was on the sabbath day. The sabbath was a day of a "shut-down" unto God. It was a day when man shut himself off from all the things of the flesh, the mind, and the soul. To be still and know God, (Isaiah 58:3). "Behold in the day of your fast ye find pleasure, and exact all your labours." (KJV). In this chapter, (Isaiah 58), the children of Israel wondered aloud why the Lord had not honored their abstinence of food. In verse 3, He says, "...WHEREFORE HAVE WE FASTED SAY THEY AND THOU SEEST NOT?

WHEREFORE HAVE WE AFFLICTED OUR SOUL, AND THOU TAKEST NO KNOWLEDGE?" (emphasis, per author). This was their concern, in other words. "We have fasted in our traditional, religious, self-righteous manner, but we have seen no results." God's response is, "...BEHOLD IN THE DAY OF

YOUR FAST YOU FIND PLEASURE AND EXACT ALL YOUR LABOURS!" (emphasis, per author). In other words, they were not really fasting, (Isaiah 58:13).

"...IF THOU TURN AWAY THY FOOT FROM THE SABBATH, FROM DOING THY PLEASURE ON MY HOLY DAY; AND CALL THE SABBATH A DELIGHT, THE HOLY OF THE HONORABLE; AND HONOR HIM, BY NOT DOING THY OWN PLEASURE, NOR SPEAKING THY OWN WORDS, (emphasis, per author). Real abstinence and fasting is a sabbath unto the Lord. In order to bring ourselves into the spirit of fasting, we must first begin to understand God's mind as it pertains to a fast.

I want to suggest that before you read this book, that you read Isaiah 58. You will then have "the spirit" of much of the rest of this book.

The City of Sodom and Fasting

In order that we may better understand fasting, we will read about a group of people who did not fast unto God, but lived according to the control of the flesh. They fasted unto and into the flesh. This may seem to be a bit strange to you, but several years ago the Lord spoke to me and said, "YOU ARE ALWAYS FASTING, YOU ARE EITHER FASTING UNTO THE FLESH OR INTO THE SPIRIT." In other words, something always has your undivided attention.

EZEKIEL 16:49-50

"...Behold this was the iniquity of thy sister Sodom, pride, fullness of bread, and abundance of idleness was in her daughter, neither did she strengthen the hand of the poor and needy, and they were haughty, and committed abominations before me: Therefore, I took them away as i saw good." (KJV).

This may surprise you, but the cause of the judgement of Sodom was other than what you may have thought. If you will notice in the above verse, it speaks of pride, fullness of bread, idleness, and no concern of the poor. What a contrast to the scripture in Isaiah 58, where it says, "...IS NOT TO DEAL THY BREAD TO THE HUNGRY, AND THAT THOU BRING THE POOR THAT ARE CAST OUT TO THY HOUSE? WHEN THOU SEEST THE NAKED, THAT THOU COVER HIM, AND THAT THY HIDE NOT THYSELF FROM THY OWN

FLESH.?" (emphasis, per author). Sodom sinned by overeating and not giving, by selfishness rather than selflessness, and an abundance of idleness. This was the real iniquity of Sodom.

It is very popular to teach that the sin of Sodom was homosexuality. The scripture shows that it was so much more than that, it was much deeper than that. It was their refusal to fast. The lack of fasting, their overeating and their selfishness was the sin. The lack of fasting from the flesh, led to fasting to the flesh; which ultimately lead to other bondages and an abomination that eventually led to God's judgement on Sodom.

1 CORINTHIANS 10:5 - 7

"But with many of them God was not well pleased: for they were overthrown in the wilderness. Now these were our examples, to the intent we should not lust after evil things, as they also lusted. Neither be ye idolaters, as were some of them; as it is written."

Again, we see the results of fasting to the flesh. The downward path of sowing to the flesh, and then reaping death. This was even seen with the children of Israel. All appetites are connected, because they all have the same origin, the soul. Esau sold his birthright for a bowl of porridge. God, grant us temperance, (See Galatians 5:23). They that are Christ's have crucified the flesh with the affections and lusts.

Fasting From Food

Fasting from food is the first consideration for most people who consider this route to take in fasting. This is commonly the practice that they understand. In the following section we will discuss different types of fasts, as we identify them from scripture.

Partial Fast

"In those days, I Daniel was mourning for three full weeks. I ate no pleasant bread, neither came flesh nor wine in my mouth, neither did I anoint myself at all til three whole weeks were fulfilled." (Daniel 10:2-3, KJV).

In this verse, Daniel was on a 21 day fast. This was not a complete fast, nor was it a normal fast, and we will discuss

this further, later in this book. In this passage we see Daniel say that he ate no pleasant bread. The word "pleasant" in Hebrew is the word 'chamudoth,' which means desirable objects. So we see that Daniel did eat food, but his selection of food was only what was needed for survival. We also see this concept repeated in Daniel

1:12, in which he was requested as a young man in the king's court to be given a short-term diet of pulse. "Prove thy servants, I beseech thee, ten days; and let them give us pulse to eat, and water to drink." (Daniel 1:12, KJV). The word "pulse" is the Hebrew word "zeoim," which means seeds. This is without question the most basic of foods. On this fast, Daniel, more than likely, ate even a very reduced ration of the pulse. He drank no wine, but rather chose water, nor did he eat flesh or meat.

This is considered a partial fast. Daniel referred to it as mourning. As we have previously seen in the book of Isaiah, fasting is called mourning. There is no question about the fact that God was well pleased with this type of fast. This is one of the most important fasts of the Bible. This fast, as all fasts do, brought forth great spiritual movement in the Spirit realm.

Michael, the Archangel himself, the great warring angel, was sent as a result of this fast. I think it is important to note here, as we see so clearly from Daniel, everything happens in the spirit realm, well before you see it manifest in the natural. This misunderstanding is the very reason why many become disappointed in fasting, because they expect to see something in the sight realm right away and when they do not, they quit the fast. I wonder what would have happened if Daniel had decided to quit only after a few days into the fast?

It was through this fast that Daniel was literally able to change the course of history. The earthly empire of the Medes and Persians was completely removed as a result of this very fast.

There is no question that partial fasting is a very powerful weapon.

One of the advantages of this type of fast is that the loss of strength and energy is not as severe as it would be if it were a complete fast or a normal fast. Although, even on a prolonged fast of nature, there will still be, in some cases, a real loss of strength, as noted in Daniel 10:8, 19. In most cases, the loss of strength is only a temporary occurrence in any long fast of any kind. The key thing to remember is that the Holy Spirit should give direction in any kind of fasting. Jesus was led of the spirit into the wilderness to fast. God, the Father, by His Spirit, lead.

CHAPTER THREE

Normal Fast

Luke 4:2

"Being forty days tempted of the devil. And in those days He ate nothing: and when they were ended, He afterward hungered." (KJV).

The reason we are referring to this as a "normal fast," is because this is the fast undertaken in scripture most frequently. We are not making a reference to the length of the fast, we will talk about that later. What we are looking at here, in terms of fasting, is that there is no food consumed at all.

There is the taking in of water. Notice in the scriptural verse, it says, "...afterward He hungered." It may interest you to ask the question, why did He hunger afterward?

You would think that the verse would say that He hungered during the fast.

The answer is this, when it comes to most fasts that exceed a 5 - 7 day window, by that time the hunger has subsided. What we want to understand here is the difference between "habit hunger" and "real hunger." I will submit to you that most Americans know nothing about real hunger. In 1 Corinthians 10:6 we read, "Now these things were our examples, to the intent that we should not lust after evil things...." This passage is in reference to the children of Israel when they made their Exodus from Egypt. When the children of Israel were in the wilderness, God fed them with manna. This manna was the angel's food, but it was not enough for them!

There is no doubt that it was enough that they would be full and they would also remain healthy, but they were not satisfied. Numbers 11:5 - 6 reads, "We remember the fish, which we did eat in Egypt freely; the cucumbers, and the melons, and the leeks, and the onions, and the garlic: But now our soul is dried away: there is nothing at all, beside this manna, before our eyes."

Notice how they said, "...but now our soul is dried away." They did not say these bodies were dried away, but their souls!!" They were unhappy because they could not satisfy habit- hunger lust. This very attitude of theirs is what brought forth God's wrath! In Numbers 11:4 we read, "WHO SHALL GIVE US FLESH TO EAT?" (emphasis, per author). Their desires came out of their "habit-hunger," not any true hunger. Yes, God has freely given His children all things to enjoy, but we must never become enslaved to any appetite. Food had surely become an idol in this case. Remember Job in Job 23:12, "...I have esteemed the words of his mouth more than my necessary food." Job had placed food in the right place in his heart.

So it is that when we go on a normal fast of any length, there will be the cessation of hunger at the point of about 6 days, that is the usual norm. At this point the stomach has shrunk. The body has begun the process of burning out the toxins and all the excesses that are in our systems. Our systems are being cleansed in a natural sense. This was the secret to Mose's health during his old age, Deut. 34:7, "And Moses was an hundred and twenty years old when he died: his eye was not dim, nor his natural force abated." This was very much the result of the great level of fasting that Moses did when he was on Mt. Sinai.

When you reach the point, during the fast, that there is no longer any hunger, fasting is much easier. It takes a real fight of faith to reach that point. You will win, however, if you stand on the promise of God that you can do all things.

Once your hunger returns, you have completed the fast. What the body has done, from the physiological standpoint, is disposed of all the toxins and waste in your system. This is then the point that hunger will return, "...AFTERWARD HE HUNGERED." (emphasis, per author). Jesus was not hungry during the fast, if so satan would have had an advantage in his temptation to get Jesus to eat.

I submit to you that once Jesus moved past the place of hunger during the first few days, it was temptation of another nature that was His challenge! I believe it was sleep and companionship that Jesus longed for during that time. I believe that Jesus spent many nights "in watch," and went without sleep. The Apostle Paul makes mention of this when he spoke of the watching often. We will not go into this topic of discussion at length here, but please let me refer you to our book entitled, "WATCHING."

During this time of fasting, Jesus was very much positioned dualistically...He was not only in a natural state, but very much positioned in the realm of the Spirit. In Mark 1:13 we are told that He was with the wild beasts during His fast. The beasts that Jesus was with were not only the beasts of the physical realm, but we need to see that it was also the beasts in the spirit, because He fought in serious spiritual battle.

These were truly fighting and opposing spirits! His fight was the great spiritual battle of forces, we read of, that He later encounters all throughout the gospels.

The Apostle Paul spoke of fighting with the beast at Ephesus. We will read a portion of this account to get a clearer understanding of this scripture. "If after the manner of men I have fought with the beast at Ephesus...." (Ephesians 15:32a). You will notice that the Apostle Paul was not in battle with lions, tigers or bears, but his battle was with demon- possessed men. So here we see that when Jesus was with the wild beasts in the wilderness, what actually transpired was a battle in the spirit, before hand, of the demon-possessed people He would later encounter in the natural. This is also a good place to mention another writing that will prove invaluable to you, and that is our book entitled, "ABSENT FROM THE BODY."

The end result of Jesus' fast is that He returned in power and demonstration of the Spirit. He was able to surely declare that "...the Spirit of the Lord is upon Me because He has anointed Me to preach the gospel." (Luke 4:18, KJV)

CHAPTER FOUR

COVENANT FASTING

Matthew 18:19 (KJV)

"Again I say unto you, that if two of you shall agree on earth as touching anything, they shall ask, it shall be done for them of my Father which is in heaven."

ACTS 23:12 (KJV)

"And when it was day, certain of the Jews banded together, and bound themselves under a curse, saying that they would neither eat nor drink till they had killed Paul."

To understand covenant fasting, we must become aware of the body nature of all of our works for the Lord. We are the body of Christ. We are dependent on one another, Romans 15:1, "We then that are strong ought to bear the infirmities of the weak, and not to please ourselves." (KJV).

When one undertakes fasting in a wrong spirit, it is dangerous because it can open the door for becoming full of spiritual pride, self-righteousness, etc. We can never think in terms of our fasts as great spiritual accomplishments that we have achieved. This is the very reason covenant fasting has such great value. On a personal note, this happens to be my favorite kind of fasting. I must take a moment to openly confess to you, my brothers and sisters, that this writer has failed many times, even those times when I have been called by the Lord into the Spirit, to lead a fast. However, on the many occasions that God called me into a covenant fast with a brother or sister, it was then that I was able to complete some of the many fasts God has called me to undertake, down through the years. This fast in particular, is a really great fast in which husbands and wives can come into agreement.

If you will notice, according to the above verse, Matthew 18:19, "...that if two shall agree on anything, it shall be done for them by My Father." (KJV). My God, what a powerful promise!! The word agree, in the Greek, is the word "SUMPHONEO," WHICH MEANS TO SPEAK OR SOUND

TOGETHER. If we stop and think about husbands and wives reading off of the same page and their speaking together, that in itself, would be a major miracle! This no doubt would bring peace into the many homes where there is strife. What better way to covenant together in a fast, since God has already covenanted to make the two, one flesh? The basis for covenant fasting is the idea that there is the support and encouragement for one another. It is good to remember that in order to successfully make it through the entire fast period, it would be best to include the entire family. This kind of fast can also be done on a corporate level, where the entire church comes together, as we read in Ezra 8:21, "Then I proclaimed a fast there at the river of Aha'va that we might afflict ourselves before our God...." Notice the usage of the pronouns, "we" and "ourselves." These were both used in the plural form, because it was a covenant fast that had been proclaimed. Another example of covenant fasting, in scripture, is listed in Acts 13:1-3a. (See scripture). In that passage we read of a covenant fast that was proclaimed in Antioch. We see a group of Prophets and teachers that have entered into fasting and prayer unto the Lord.

Joel 1:14 (KJV)

"Sanctify ye a fast, call a solemn assembly, gather the elders, and all the inhabitants of the land into the house of the Lord your God and cry unto the Lord."

This fast in Joel, is a covenant, corporate fast. Joel is a book written with regard to restoration for Israel. All that we see that happens in the book of Joel, centers around the spirit of restoration. Part of the restoration process for the church is covenant fasting. This is the kind of fast that will break down the walls of the flesh and will knit hearts together. If you take another look at Acts 13:1, you will see that it is a group of Prophets and teachers that have entered into a fast. A closer look at the scripture, you will see that it is an interracial group that has come together in this fast, it is an interracial church.

This was made possible simply because the spirit of fasting has the ability to break down those walls and barriers of racial bias, which is an unfortunate stronghold, in the church of today.

Proclaimed Fast

Joel 2;15 & 16

"Blow the trumpet in Zion, sanctify a fast, call a solemn assembly: Gather the people, sanctify the congregation, assemble the elders, gather the children, and those that suck the breast...." (KJV).

This scripture in Joel, speaks of the terrible spiritual condition of the church. The palmerworm, the locusts, the cankerworm, and the caterpillars have eaten the truths away from the church. The new wine is cut off. The new wine is the representation of the Holy Spirit. This says the gifts of the Holy Spirit are not in operation. This speaks to a great need in the church for restoration in absolutely every area. In the book of Joel, we read a continual reference to the locusts. Locust, as seen in the Old Testament, is almost always a reference to destruction and erosion. Locusts are seen in the Old Testament as the judgment of God. Locusts are known to multiply, as they are slowly eating away plant life and vegetation, etc. What a clear picture the Holy Spirit is able to portray of the condition of today's church.

The one and only spiritual remedy for this sad state of affairs, is fasting, a chastening of the soul. Joel declares that a trumpet needed to be sounded in Zion. In other words, the ministers, who are the trumpet blowers, need to cry out and proclaim a fasting in their congregations. If it is not in the congregations, then it needs to be wherever they, as ministers, are stationed on the wall. A cry needs to be made for fasting in order to bring restoration to God's people.

We see that in both Joel 1:14 and in Joel 2:15 & 16 it calls for a solemn assembly. The word SOLEMN comes from the Hebrew word, ASTERETH. This means to restrain. In other words it calls for the people to come together, sit down, shut- up and listen to what the Spirit has to say. How many times has this writer been in gatherings of God's people where singing, shouting and praising is the only agenda? Fasting is a time of breaking, a time of breaking up the fallow ground, which we read about in Hosea 10:12. This is a time of sowing to yourselves in righteousness. Praise and worship, no doubt has it's place in the purposes of God, but if we are to be lead of the Spirit, even as it pertains to praise and worship, we are better able to praise and worship, as the Holy Spirit leads us to do so, through fasting. This is reflected in the scripture we read in Ecclesiastes 5:1, which says, "Keep thy foot when thy goest to the house of God, and be more ready to hear, than to give the sacrifice of fools: for they consider not that they do evil." (KJV). When the verse says "Keep thy foot," it is stating that God wants you to allow Him to move you, versus you moving yourself. We are not to follow patterns, traditions, or even the action of others. Be quick to hear, first and foremost. We should want to wait on messages in tongues, to be interpreted; as well as to wait on prophesy to come forth instead of rushing right into another chorus or another song.

Never mind moving onto the next thing on the agenda! When we start right up with praising and worshipping to God, when not lead of the Holy Spirit, and the Holy Spirit is desirous of tongues and interpretation, as well as prophesy; then we offer the sacrifice of fools. MY God!! How many, many times have I seen and witnessed this? This behavior brings such tremendous grief to the heart of God. We need ministers to proclaim solemn assembly's and fast times unto the Lord.

The word PROCLAIM comes from the Hebrew word ABAR.

This word means to "cause to pass over." There is an issue with regard to authority implied here. MINISTERS, USE YOUR AUTHORITY - - - PASTORS, TEACHERS, PROPHETS & APOSTLES...proclaim a fast!! Cause your voice to pass over. In 2 Chronicles 20:3 - 4 we read where Jehoshaphat proclaimed a fast. This was called when the children of Ammon, Moab and others came against the children of Judah. If you read this account carefully, you will see that a solemn assembly was called. The first order of business, as we read in the 4th verse, is that they gathered themselves together. After they were gathered, they then asked for help from the Lord!

How we need to see a restoration of proclaimed fasting in the church. Let's face it ministers, we proclaim everything else.

WE SAY THAT GOD SAID TO BUILD NEW BUILDINGS, PARKING LOTS, BUY NEW CHOIR ROBES, RAISE MORE MONEY, etc. WHY NOT PROCLAIM A FAST? If ministers would begin to proclaim fasts in the church, it would change the world!!

Another point we want to emphasize here is that the assembly included the elders. Ministers need to come together in fasting and prayer. If they did so, it would break down all kinds of walls, all kinds of barriers that exist between churches, ministers, denominations, etc. It is of the utmost importance that ministers lead by example in fasting and prayer. As a minister, if you do not fast much on a personal basis, do not expect the people of your assembly to fast, it has to first start with you.

Jonah 3:5 (KJV)

"So the people of Nineveh believed God, and proclaimed a fast, and put on sackcloth, from the greatest of them even to the least of them."

In this story of Jonah, we see an entire nation saved through the proclamation of a fast. I submit to you, that in repentance to God, many famines are probably "forced fasts" that God will sometimes allow as acts of mercy that spawns repentance of a people. Nineveh was set for the judgment of God. Jonah was sent to warn them of this impending judgment. The king of Nineveh, himself, was the one that proclaimed the fast. He was equivalent to what would be the president, in our nation, of the U.S.A. It is historically documented that President Abraham Lincoln proclaimed public national fasting days, as well as President George Washington. To proclaim times of national fasting is very much a part of the historical culture of this country as well as others. It is good to have a history of walking in the blessing of God.

CHAPTER SIX

SPIRITUAL LIGHT

Revelation 1:10

The Apostle John said, "I was in the spirit on the Lord's day."

I believe John was in a fasting and prayer mode of function at this time, on the Lord's day. It was during this time that John received the many great visions which he wrote about, that make up the book of Revelations. In the Greek, the word REVELATION is the word, APOKALUPISIS. This word means to unveil or uncover. We want to get a different perspective on the actual word, "revelation." We have talked about revelation as it pertains to the natural realm, let us now take a look at revelation, as it pertains to spiritual truths.

All truths are parallel. Just as in the natural realm there are times of natural breakthroughs, so it is that there are times of spiritual breakthroughs that are purely spiritual. Peter was in fasting and prayer when he fell into a trance and received the truth that the Gentiles were to be saved. This was revelation about hidden spiritual truths. The church is on the threshold of tremendous spiritual revelation. We are coming into the hour of the open vision. The open vision is the highest form of vision in which a man can walk. The veil or cover is ripped away, in order for spiritual things or truths to be seen as clearly as anything in the natural could be seen. Peter said in the book of Acts, "I SAW HEAVEN OPENED...." (emphasis, per author, KJV). As Peter fasted and pressed through to the revelation of God's purposes in the church, he took the church into a new era. This came in fasting and prayer! God always sends the revelation before He sends the acts. The reason so many works and acts of the church are dead and lifeless, is because they were not born out of revelation. "Surely the Lord God will do nothing, but he revealeth his secret unto his servants the prophets." (Amos 3:7, KJV). We do not need anymore man-made programs. We need the revelation of God's program.

Jesus told His disciples that He had many things to tell them that they were not yet able to bear. How were they to receive these truths that He had not yet committed to them? They would receive them by revelation! Do you believe there is yet revelation within the scriptures that we have not yet discovered? Maybe you do not believe this to be so, but I certainly do! My heart is tired of the old and dried up traditions.

When you fast, you bring your spirit into a place that allows you to receive revelation. It is important to keep in mind, the revelation flows out of your spirit. This is why the Holy Spirit spoke to the psalmist these words, "...be still and know that I am God." (Psalm 46:10a, KJV). When you purpose to bring your mind and your soul into a place of quiet, through fasting, you are then able to receive out of your spirit-man. his is just one of the forms by which revelation comes. Earlier, we spoke of the fact that light is suppressed by darkness. What is darkness and what is the devil and his powers, but those evil forces that stand against all insightful revelation. The very last thing the devil wants to see happen is that any person learn more about God! The devil is opposed to any and all light, but no satanic power is opposed to religion!! As a matter of fact, the devil loves religion! But, he certainly hates revelation!

When Daniel was on his 21 day fast, his end result was that he received revelation, great revelation! Notice the words spoken by the angel in Daniel 9:23, "AT THE BEGINNING OF THY SUPPLICATIONS THE COMMANDMENT CAME FORTH, AND I AM COME TO SHEW; FOR THOU ART GREATLY BELOVED: THEREFORE UNDERSTAND THE MATTER, AND CONSIDER THE VISION." (emphasis per author, KJV). This angel had come in order to give Daniel understanding and to give to him the truth. In reading the balance of the book of Daniel, you will find that some of the greatest prophetic truths of scripture were revealed to Daniel during his time.

I have discovered that even when it comes to bible study, that does not result in revelation to your spirit, turns out to be rather boring. When Moses was on Mt. Sinai, in fasting for 40 days, the end result was that the revelation he received was so tremendous, that it prompted Moses to therefore ask God if he could see Him!

Your entire relationship with God is based on revelation. Christ in you is a revelation. This is why Jesus told Peter in Matthew 16:18, "UPON THIS ROCK WILL I BUILD MY CHURCH AND THE GATES OF HELL SHALL NOT PREVAIL

AGAINST IT." (emphasis, per author,KJV). The rock that Jesus made reference to, was the rock of revelation to your spirit-man that "Jesus is Lord."

We are living in the hour of the increase of knowledge in every realm of existence. Get ready to see more and more breakthroughs come forth. These breakthroughs will not always come to some well known Christian leader, either. God will speak to anyone that is willing to pay the price to hear. The knowledge of God is equally available to any and everyone. I will never forget about the time in which I was in prison, in 1991, I was listening to God as He brought forth wonderful revelation. It was truth out of the Word of God. I thought in my heart that it would be good to share this revelation with some of the brothers. The Holy Spirit spoke to my heart and said, "GET YOUR OWN REVELATION." Praise God! No one has to ride on anyone else's anointing, it is up to that person to get their own. Pay the price. So much of the revelation of God has not been received, merely because it cancels out the power of the pride and glory of man getting it through his own mind and intellect! This very fact is the basis for why Jesus prayed in Luke 10:21a and said, "I THANK THEE, O FATHER, LORD OF HEAVEN AND EARTH, THAT THOU HAST HID THESE THINGS FROM THE WISE AND PRUDENT...." (emphasis, per author, KJV). We will miss so much revelation light if we refuse to humble ourselves. This is the very reason why so many people stumble. If it is speaking in tongues, they allow their minds to get in the way; so they conclude it to be foolishness. The natural man always sees things as foolishness. This is why through the process of fasting, as you come to a place of humility before God, you will then be able to see, understand and receive the revelation of the spirit.

Let me also state clearly here, all revelation does not come as a bolt of lightning. Revelation is also able to unfold through a gradual process, as you read, study, pray and grow. My experience has been that as God gives revelation, it would be as He would sometimes drop the revelation of 'some truth ' into a person's spirit, and then He will begin to develop this truth in that person, as they follow on to know the truth. I can reasonably say, we have received much revelation from God that came by fasting and prayer. I tell you two words of revelation from God is sweeter than one hundred dried-up hours of traditions of unbelief and fear.

Proverbs 4:18

"But the path of the just, is as the shining light, that shineth more and more unto the perfect day." (KJV).

CHAPTER SEVEN

FASTING OFTEN

2Corinthians 12:27 (KJV)

"In weariness and painfulness, in watching often, in hunger and thirst, in fasting often, in cold and nakedness."

Paul speaks of frequent fasting. This type of fasting is the type practiced in between protracted fasts. This is living the fasted lifestyle. Paul also spoke of bringing his body under subjection, in the following verse:

1 Corinthians 9:27 (KJV)

"But I keep under my body, and bring it into subjection: lest that by any means, when I have preached to others, I myself should be a castaway."

The word KEEP here is the Greek word HUPOPIAZO, which means to keep down or to press under. There are some believers who have been lead of the Spirit into perpetual fasts. That is, they decide to give up specific meals perpetually. Some believers will fast from 6 am until 6 pm, perpetually. Through this practice, they keep the body under, as they live in a continual fasted mode. These persons are then able to be instant in season and out of season. No doubt, Jesus practiced this kind of fasting. He was always in a fast mode. He was a living dead man. The reason the disciples were unable to cast out the deaf and dumb spirit in Mark 9 is because they were not living a fasted lifestyle. Mark 9:29 says, "...this kind can come forth by nothing, but by prayer and fasting." (KJV). Jesus was not saying that the disciples needed to go on a fast of a specific length, in order to cast out this kind of spirit. There are no spirits specifically identified in the scriptures, that requires fasting in order to come out. What Jesus was dealing with, however, was the spiritual condition of the disciples. Their hearts were not filled with faith, because they were not living fasted lives. Therefore, when we fast often, it prompts us to be filled with faith. Romans 10:17 says, "So then faith cometh by hearing, and hearing by the word of God."

CHAPTER EIGHT

FASTING AND SPIRITUAL WARFARE

Ephesians 6:12 (KJV)

"For we wrestle not against flesh and blood, but against principalities, against powers, against the rulers of darkness of this world, against spiritual wickedness in high places."

2 Corinthians 10: 3 - 4 (KJV)

"For though we walk in the flesh, we do not war after the flesh: For the weapons of our warfare are not carnal, but mighty through God to the pulling down of strongholds   "

In Ephesians 6, the Apostle Paul gives us information about with who we, as Christians, are in a fight. In 2

Corinthians 10:3-4, the Apostle Paul speaks of how we fight. First and foremost he wants us to recognize that the battle is purely spiritual. We are not fighting mortal man, but the spirits that operate through man. These spiritual entities cannot be fought with the power of human hands, men's programs or by any other carnal means. Paul said that even though we walk in the flesh, we do not war after the flesh. God has committed spiritual warfare to His church. He has given us the weapons we are to use. One of the greatest of these weapons is fasting and prayer. In order to have the right perspective of the value of this weapon, let us take a look at how one Old Testament, spiritual warrior used these weapons. (Read Daniel, Chapter 10). In this chapter, Daniel went on a 21 day fast. His purpose was to petition God in behalf of the people of Israel. Israel had been taken into captivity, in Babylon, seventy years earlier.

Daniel had read in the book of the Prophet Jeremiah, the following:

"FOR THUS SAITH THE LORD, THAT AFTER SEVENTY YEARS BE ACCOMPLISHED AT BABYLON I WILL VISIT YOU; AND PERFORM MY GOOD WORD TOWARDS YOU, CAUSING

YOU TO RETURN TO THIS PLACE." (Jeremiah 29:10, KJV).

God had promised to deliver His people, Israel. Daniel, therefore, set his face to fast and pray. Daniel 9:3, "And I set my face UNTO THE LORD GOD; TO SEEK BY PRAYER SUPPLICATIONS; WITH FASTING; AND SACKCLOTH AND ASHES." (emphasis, per author, KJV).

Daniel made a decision to go on a fast in order to seek God's fulfillment of the prophecy. On the 21st day, an angel appeared to him, (verse 5). In verses 12-13, the angel informed Daniel of the fact that his prayer had been heard from the very first day. His words were heard when he fasted and prayed. The angel was then dispatched from heaven, but the angel of the Lord was withstood by a fallen angel, a prince of the devil, which is one of the principalities that Paul speaks of in Ephesians 6. Daniel continues to prevail, however, in fasting and prayer, which results in God dispatching help, this being in the form of Michael, one of the chief princes. Michael helped to bring the breakthrough in the spirit realm. You will notice, that in verse 20, Michael gives details of the spiritual events that had served to overshadow the natural events. He gives insight on the removal of the Prince of Persia and the coming of the Prince of Grecia. Michael was speaking of the end of the reign of the Medes and Persians, when they were conquered by the Greeks and Alexander the Great. We know this to be a true historical event, all of which first took place in the realm of the spirit, because of fasting and prayer. Daniel's fast actually changed the course of recorded history!! The defeat of the Medes Persian Empire by Alexander the Great is a historical fact. From this account alone, we can see that fasting is a very, very powerful weapon in spiritual warfare.

Numbers 21:14

"Wherefore it is said in the book of the wars
of the Lord, What he did in the Red Sea and
in the brooks of Arnon...." (KJV).

God has a spiritual book in heaven, the book called the Book of the Wars of the Lord. This is a book in which all the recording angels record all the great spiritual warfares and battles that have been waged by God's people. To this very day, these same kinds of battles are still fought in the realm of the spirit. Just as there are authentic battles fought even today, among nations, many of these battles are fought through the power of ones that are led to fast for these battles.

PROPHECY

This saith the Lord, "Yea, even know that there are great battles being fought in the Spirit realm, saith the Lord. Yea, wars that you see not. Yea, they are wars that are more real than the wars on earth. Yea, every event on earth is first decided in the realm of the Spirit.

Yea, in many areas, My great angels of war stand, yea, with their very hands tied, yea, because My people are dormant. Yea, the church is still asleep. Yea, they are living in the flesh and living in pleasure, saith the Lord. Yea, they will not fast unto Me, because their hearts and minds are filled with the love of the things of this hour.

Yea, but I shall raise up an army of hidden warriors, and they shall fast into the battle and bring down every stronghold of the devil. Yea, My people, if you only knew the power I have invested in thee. Yea, even as Moses and Daniel, under the Old Covenant, changed the course of human events, so shall you in this time of grace, saith the Lord. If you will but give your bodies to Me, in fasting and prayer.

Yea, know, yea not that even the walls of communism were pulled down by fasting and prayer? Yea, know the Berlin Wall came down, yea, as My little ones gave their bodies to Me in fasting and prayer., saith the Lord. Yea, this is the hour of restoration of all things. I will do the work in this hour, that is yet to be done in the earth. Yea, all that you have read in the scriptures shall be a small thing in comparison to what I shall do in this last hour. Yea I will call you by My Spirit to fast, to fast and pray. Yea, as you read these words that I have given unto My servant, know that these words are sent to give light and revelation and insight; if you will receive them, saith the Lord."

NOTES

Other Books Written By: Chief
Apostle Joseph L. Prude

Prophetic Laboratory Office of the Dream Master

Dream Masters College Curriculum Female Apostle

The False Bishop

Restoring Healing in The African
American Church The Creation

Ministry of the Apostle Office of the Chief
Apostle Ministry of the Prophet

Ministry of the Prophet Level 2 The Certified
Prophetic Trainer The Highjacking of the
Gospel The Secrets of His Presence

The Mystery of Angels

The False Teaching of the Tallit How to
Interpret Any Dream Interracial Marriage

Prophetic Proverbs

The Ministry of Fasting and Prayer

josephprude@gmail.com Order
books on amazon.com or

www.ajpministries.com

www.ingramcontent.com/pod-product-compliance
Lightning Source LLC
Chambersburg PA
CBHW030830060726
47590CB00004B/1470